I ♥

KOALAS

Buster Books

Illustrated by
Lizzie Preston and
Sarah Wade

Edited by Imogen Currell-Williams
Designed by Derrian Bradder

A percentage of the proceeds from
the sale of this book will be donated
to charities helping to care for injured
koalas and other wildlife affected
by the devastating bushfires
in Australia.

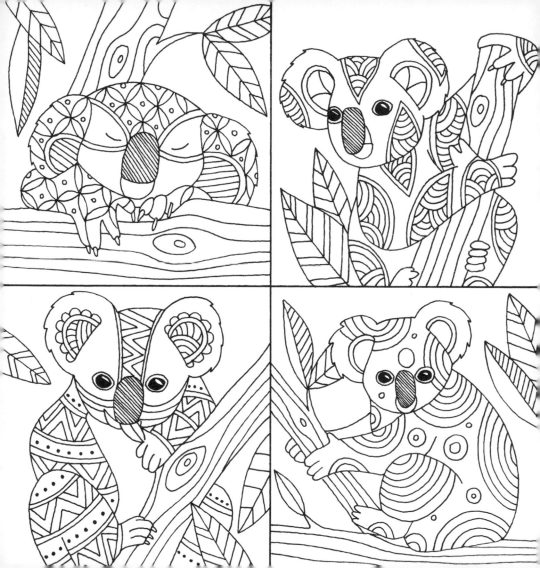

First published in Great Britain in 2020 by Buster Books,
an imprint of Michael O'Mara Books Limited, 9 Lion Yard,
Tremadoc Road, London SW4 7NQ

W www.mombooks.com/buster   f Buster Books   🐦 @BusterBooks

Copyright © Buster Books 2020

With additional material adapted from www.shutterstock.com

All rights reserved. No part of this book may be reproduced, stored
in a retrieval system, or transmitted in any form or by any means,
without the prior permission in writing of the publisher.

ISBN: 978-1-78055-725-0

2 4 6 8 10 9 7 5 3 1

This book was printed in June 2020 by
Shenzhen Wing King Tong Paper Products Co. Ltd.,
Shenzhen, Guangdong, China.

MIX
Paper from
responsible sources
FSC® C010256
FSC
www.fsc.org